The Past Tells a Story

Lorna Evans

MACMILLAN

© Copyright text Lorna Evans 1996
© Copyright illustrations Macmillan Education Ltd 1996

All rights reserved. No reproduction, copy or transmission of this publication may be made without written permission.

No paragraph of this publication may be reproduced, copied or transmitted save with written permission or in accordance with the provisions of the Copyright, Designs and Patents Act 1988, or under the terms of any licence permitting limited copying issued by the Copyright Licensing Agency, 90 Tottenham Court Road, London W1P 9HE.

Any person who does any unauthorised act in relation to this publication may be liable to criminal prosecution and civil claims for damages.

First published 1996

Published by MACMILLAN EDUCATION LTD
London and Basingstoke
Associated companies and representatives in Accra, Banjul, Cairo, Dar es Salaam, Delhi, Freetown, Gaborone, Harare, Hong Kong, Johannesburg, Kampala, Lagos, Lahore, Lusaka, Mexico City, Nairobi, São Paulo, Tokyo

ISBN 0-333-61117-9

Printed in Hong Kong

A catalogue record for this book is available from the British Library.

Series editor: Lorna Evans

Acknowledgements

The authors and publishers wish to acknowledge, with thanks, the following photographic sources:
Ardea pp7 (photograph Mina Carpi); 13 below (photograph P Morris); 18 above left (photograph P J Green); 18 above right (photograph P Morris); 18 centre (photograph P J Green); 14 (photograph Jean-Michel Labat)
Science Photograph Library pp2 (photograph David Hardy);
 3 (photograph Ludek Pesek); 13 above (photograph Alfred Pasieka);
 21 (photograph John Reader); 27 (photograph John Reader);
 33 (photograph John Reader)
The cover photograph is courtesy of Science Photograph Library/David A Hardy
Illustrations by Edna Moore

The publishers have made every effort to trace the copyright holders, but if they have inadvertently overlooked any, they will be pleased to make the necessary arrangements at the first opportunity.

A Long Time Ago

In the beginning there was one God. His name was Amma, and he made the stars, the Sun, the Moon and the Earth.

First Amma threw tiny pieces of clay high into the sky, and these formed the stars.

To make the Earth he squeezed a lump of clay into a ball and threw it into the sky as well.

Next he threw a bigger piece of clay amongst the stars. This clay formed the Sun. It was white hot, and around the Sun there were eight rings of red copper.

Then Amma made the Moon from a smaller piece of clay. Around the Moon there were eight rings of white copper.

Much later, after many troubles, Amma made men and women to live on the earth.

Is this really how the Earth was formed and how life began?

If you had lived in one part of West Africa a hundred years ago, your parents would have told you this story. Parents in different parts of Africa would have told different tales. And in the rest of the world there were even more stories.

Today scientists can tell us more about what really happened.

The Earth probably looked like this when it was first formed. Today it is cooler and has a crust of hard rock around it.

This is probably what the Earth looked like about two million years ago.(opposite)

Part 1

Life on Earth

How the Earth was formed

The Earth was formed about 4600 million years ago. At first it was a great hot ball of dust and gas spinning round the Sun. It was very, very hot, and quite different from the Earth we know today. There were no mountains or valleys or deserts or seas, and nothing could live on it.

The Earth cooled slowly, and as it did so a crust of hard rock formed round it. In some places the crust is 60 kilometres thick, in other places it is only three kilometres thick. Deep below its crust the Earth is still hotter than fire.

As the Earth cooled, steam and gas broke through the crust. The steam and gas turned into thick clouds which then dropped rain back on the Earth. The rain filled the hollows in the Earth's crust and formed the first seas. All this took millions and millions of years.

Changes

Millions of years ago the Earth had just one, very large continent. About 180 million years ago this continent started to break up into five smaller ones. These continents, the ones we know today, are still moving slowly away from each other, colliding with each other or moving side by side. As the continents moved they pushed up high mountains in some places, and made deep valleys in others.

There have been many other changes to the Earth's crust since it was first formed. Ice and rain broke up the rocks of the Earth's crust into smaller pieces. Streams and rivers wore away the land and washed away rocks and soil. Wind carried fine dust across deserts or far out to sea. Waves from the sea wore away the cliffs. Sometimes hot dust and rocks and gases broke through the crust as volcanoes.

The climate of the Earth has changed too. It has not always been the same. Sometimes it has been hot and wet or hot and dry. At other times it has been very cold. For millions of years much of the southern part of Africa lay below a great sheet of ice. For the last two million years the Earth has had a rather cool climate, but it may get warmer again.

All these changes are still going on, though we cannot see them. Land which was once below the sea might now be a high mountain. Land which was once a rich green valley might now be a dry desert. Land which was once buried under sheets of ice might now be a warm forest. A million years from now the Earth will look quite different from the way it looks today.

Evolution

The things which live on Earth have changed too.

For millions of years there was no life on the Earth. There were no plants or animals or birds or fish.

About 3200 million years ago tiny blue-green algae developed. Algae are very small, very simple water plants which live in water. Algae were the first living things.

All other living things have evolved from algae. The way in which new forms of life develop is called evolution. Living things change slowly over many years to adapt to different habitats.

New species are evolving and old ones are dying out all the time.

Elephants can show how evolution works. Different species of elephant adapted in different ways to their habitats.

The ancestor of the elephants lived in Africa over 40 million years ago. It was the same size as a pig and it had a very short trunk.

From Africa the elephant family spread over the whole Earth. Elephants lived in many different habitats. New species of elephant evolved as they adapted to different habitats.

The elephants became bigger and bigger. The biggest of all was over four metres high. This species became big and strong so that it could push small trees over and feed on them.

The elephants grew longer and longer upper lips. These long upper lips developed into trunks. This species used its trunk to pull down high branches from the trees so that it could eat the leaves.

The elephants developed front teeth which pointed forwards, grew longer, and became tusks. Some species used their tusks as weapons. Most species had one pair of tusks which grew from the upper jaw.

Some species of elephant even developed two pairs of tusks.

One species developed tusks which pointed downwards. They probably used their tusks to dig up roots to eat.

Some elephants spread right into the coldest places on the Earth. When this happened a new species adapted by growing a woolly coat. The woolly coat kept the elephant warm in a cold habitat.

There are only two species of elephant left today, the African elephant and the Indian elephant. The others have all died out.

Humans and evolution

Two hundred million years ago there were birds, fish, animals, and insects on the Earth, but they were very different from the species which are alive today.

Humans are a species which evolved only about three million years ago. Scientists do not understand exactly how humans evolved. They do know that our ancestors were very different from humans today.

Humans are primates, like monkeys and apes. All primates
- have large brains.
- have long arms and legs with five fingers and toes.
- have eyes which face forwards.
- have small noses.

The first primates evolved about 65 million years ago. They were small and probably lived in the trees. They were about 40 centimetres long and ate fruit, eggs, and insects.

This primate lived in Egypt about 27 million years ago. It looked like a small ape with a short tail. It lived in the trees and ate fruit. It weighed about four kilograms.

This primate stood on two legs, but probably used its arms to climb. It lived about 20 million years ago in Africa, Asia and Europe.

These species died out millions of years ago, but other species evolved and took their place. Scientists think apes and humans evolved from the same ancestor.

This species is probably a recent ancestor of humans. It lived about ten million years ago in Africa, Asia and Europe. It was about 1.2 metres high and weighed about 14 kilograms. It lived in open grassland and could stand on two legs.

We shall look at other, more recent, human ancestors later in this book.

Part 2

Fossils

How do we know so much about evolution? There were no humans on Earth until about three million years ago. Nobody saw what happened. Nobody wrote books or took photographs.

We know about evolution because when a living thing dies it does not always disappear. Sometimes it turns into a fossil.

Fossils can be found almost anywhere on the Earth today. When fossils are found they tell us about plants, birds or animals which lived millions of years ago.

This is what scientists believe the brachiosaurus looked like. The species died out millions of years ago.

A True Story

One hundred and thirty million years ago a huge brachiosaurus lived in what is now Tanzania. It was 40 feet long. It weighed nearly 100 tons, as much as 40 elephants.

The habitat of the brachiosaurus was the mouth of a big river. When the brachiosaurus died its body fell into the water.

Fish ate the soft part of the body of the brachiosaurus. Only its bones were left. These were slowly buried in the mud at the edge of the river.

Millions of years passed. The river dropped silt and mud many feet deep above the bones of the brachiosaurus. In time the layers of mud and silt and the bones of the brachiosaurus all turned into solid rock. The brachiosaurus became a fossil.

In 1907 a workman noticed some strange stones on the ground. They were the fossil bones of the brachiosaurus, exposed for the first time in 130 million years.

The bones were excavated by a team of 150 workers. They found the complete skeleton of the brachiosaurus.

Scientists cleaned and put together the bones of the brachiosaurus. This is what they look like today.

How are fossils formed?

Fossils are formed when the bodies of dead things turn into rock. This takes millions of years.

This animal lived 150 million years ago. It died near to a river, and its body fell into the water. ▶

The body of the animal was attacked and eaten by fish. The soft parts that were not eaten just rotted away. Only the bones were left. ▶

The bones of the animal lay at the bottom of the river. Soon they were buried under mud and sand. ▶

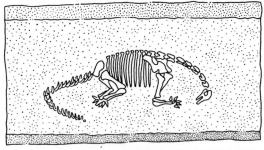

Time passed and more and more layers of mud and sand were laid down above the bones of the animal. Over millions of years the bones as well as the mud and sand turned into hard rock. The bones became fossils. ▶

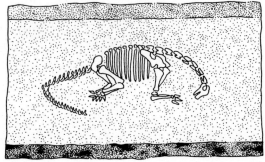

Any living thing, plant or bird or animal or insect or fish, can become a fossil. The oldest fossils are about 350 million years old.

This fossil fish lived about 50 million years ago in a warm sea.

The plant on which this leaf grew was alive about 300 million years ago when the Earth's climate was warm and wet.

This nest of eggs was laid by a reptile about 100 million years ago.

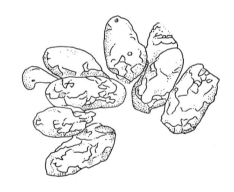

Scientists can remove fossil bones from the rock with these tools.

How are fossils exposed?

Fossils are formed deep in the Earth's crust, under layers of rock many metres deep.
- Sometimes changes to the Earth's crust expose fossils.
- A river or the sea may wear away the land so that a fossil is exposed.
- The land may rise, and wind and rain may wear away the rocks around the fossil.
- The land may be folded upwards, and again wind and rain may expose the fossil.

Where are fossils found?

The best places to find fossils are where bare rocks are exposed. Cliffs, deep river valleys, deserts and steep mountain sides are all good places to look.

Fossils often fall to the ground below from cliffs and hillsides, so the bottom of a cliff, a beach, or the bed of a river are also good places for fossils.

Sometimes people expose fossils when they dig into the earth for new buildings or roads, or to dig out quarries.

Fossils are easy to find if the fossil hunter knows what to look for. The fossil may be a different colour from the rocks around it. It may be shiny. Its shape may show up clearly.

If a fossil is found in a cliff, the fossil hunter uses a hammer to break away the rock in which he has found the fossil. If the fossil is in a piece of rock which has already broken he can just carry it away.

Some fossils are found on the ground. The fossil hunter often only sees a small part of the whole fossil at first. Sometimes he can remove the rock and soil around the fossil with a brush. Sometimes he has to break away the piece of rock in which the fossil is buried.

Sometimes thousands of fossils are found in one site. If the fossils are interesting and important a team of fossil hunters will excavate the site.

One team of fossil hunters excavated 32,000 fossils at a site in Tanzania. It took them four years to do so. They made maps to show where every fossil was found. They marked and took photographs of every fossil.

The fossil hunter is cleaning human fossil bones.

Caring for fossils

Many fossils are broken before the fossil hunters find them. Others break later, when they are moved or cleaned. The fossil hunters have to be very careful. They must always pack fossils in newspaper and strong boxes before they carry them away.

Fossil hunters usually take important fossils to museums. There, scientists clean away the rock in which the fossils are buried. Then everybody can study them.

Fossil hunters almost never find a whole fossil skeleton. Other animals attack the body when it dies, or water may carry the bones far away.

Sometimes fossil hunters do find all, or most of, the bones from one animal. Then scientists can put the bones together and see what the animal was really like.

What can we learn from fossils?

Fossils tell us a lot about the species from which they came.

If scientists have several fossil bones from one animal they can put them together and decide what the animal looked like.

The shape of fossil bones and the way they fit together tell us how animals used their bodies. The hip, leg and toe bones of animals which walk on two legs are different from the ones which walk on four. The finger bones of animals which use their hands to grip are different from those which do not.

A fossil tooth can tell us how old the animal was when it died. If the teeth are very worn the animal was probably old when it died.

A fossil tooth can also tell us what the animal ate. If the tooth is sharp and pointed the animal was probably a meat eater. It used its teeth to kill other animals and tear their bodies apart. If the tooth is broad and flat the animal was probably a plant eater. It used its teeth to crush and chew plants.

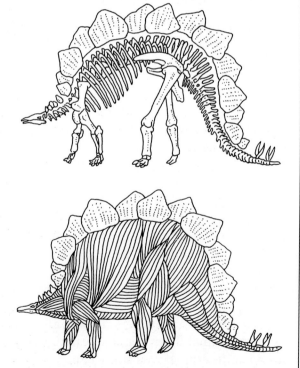

Scientists can put together fossil bones and make a whole skeleton. They do not often find every single bone from a skeleton.

Bumps and other marks on the fossil show how the muscles were fixed to the bones and how they worked.

Fossil hunters have actually found a few pieces of fossil skin. They tell us whether the skin was rough or smooth, or hairy.

How old are fossils?

The oldest fossil that has ever been found is about 2,800 million years old. It is an algae and comes from Africa.

Scientists can find out how old a fossil is. They have several ways of doing this.
- They can use special apparatus to work out the age of the rocks in which a fossil was found. The fossil will be the same age as the rocks in which it was buried.
- They can look at other fossils found nearby. If they know the age of these fossils then they can guess the age of the new one.

Fossils and evolution

Fossils can also tell us about evolution. If scientists have a lot of bones from one species they can compare them. They can look at small changes and differences between fossils. Then they can work out how an animal has evolved from its ancestors.

The horse has slowly evolved from a small animal which lived in the forest to a much bigger one which ran wild on the grasslands. Today the horse has only one toe and a hoof on each foot. It also has big strong teeth to eat hard grass.

Fifty-five million years ago the ancestor of the horse looked like this. It was the same size as a dog, and had feet with four toes which can be seen in the picture of its skeleton. Its habitat was the forest. There the ground was soft, so it needed big feet. It ate the leaves of trees and small bushes.

Forty million years ago the horse was bigger and had only three toes. It had moved away from the forest to a new habitat in the grasslands. Here the ground was harder and it did not need such big feet.

Twenty-five million years ago the horse was well-adapted to running. It ate grass. It walked on its middle toe, and its feet were very small and light.

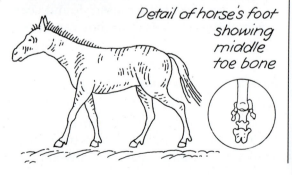

Detail of horse's foot showing middle toe bone

Part 3

Lucy

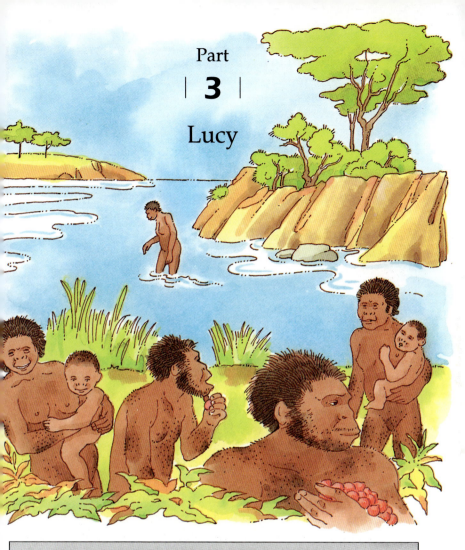

What happened to Lucy?

It was late afternoon and they were feeding by the lake. There were about 40 of them in the group, males and females. Many of the mothers carried their young. They probably lived together all their lives.

They were careful to stay on the sand bank at the edge of the lake. The deeper water in the middle was dangerous.

The sun shone down on them, as it had done all day. It had not rained for many weeks, but the air felt heavy. The storm would come soon.

> They were all hungry. The nuts and berries which they ate were hard to find. Two days before one of the males had found the body of a wild pig. They had all eaten the meat, but now they were hungry again.
>
> One of the females dragged behind the rest of the group as they looked for food. She was not very old, and she was not sick, but she was very tired and thirsty. She wanted to drink some cool water.
>
> None of them noticed as she made her way into the lake. None of them noticed as she caught her foot and fell. She was all alone when she died.
>
> Her body lay in the water at the edge of the lake.
>
> That night the rain came at last, and after that the water rose. In a few days the body was buried below a thin layer of sand and silt.

Soon after the female died a volcano threw thick clouds of dust into the air. The ash and lava from the volcano covered her body and everything else around.

Millions of years passed. The climate changed and became wetter. Heavy rain fell and the lake grew bigger. Fast rivers carried their loads of fine sand and silt into it.

The ash and lava from the volcano and the sand and silt from the river hardened into layers of rock. In time the layers of rock were over 50 metres deep. The bones themselves became fossils.

Much later the climate became dry again and the lake dried up. Today it is a desert of bare rock and sand. It is called Afar, and is in the north of Ethiopia.

It almost never rains in Afar, but when the rain does come, it is heavy. Water fills the rivers, and they cut deep gullies into the earth below.

After one great storm in Afar some fossil bones were exposed in the side of a gully. The bones were those of the female who died by the lake. They are some of the most exciting and interesting fossils ever found.

The scientists who found the bones called the female Lucy.

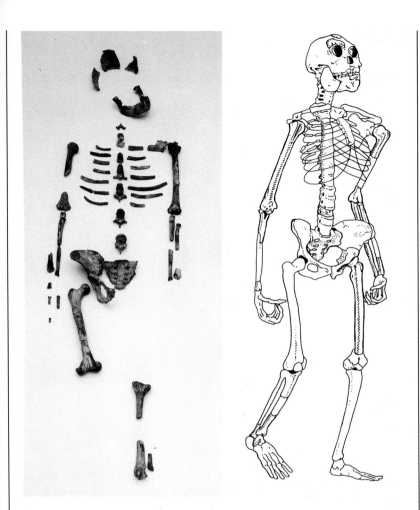

The scientists found several hundred fossil bones, many of them tiny. When they put them all together they had nearly half of Lucy's skeleton. The fossil bones came from both left and right sides of the body. It was easy for the scientists to work out what the whole skeleton looked like.

What did the scientists find?

Finding so many of Lucy's bones was very important. It does not happen very often. Usually scientists only find a few bones from one skeleton.

Lucy was found in Ethiopia. Scientists have found more fossils from the species which Lucy belonged to in other parts of Ethiopia and in Tanzania.

What was Lucy?

Lucy was a primate who lived about 3.5 million years ago. The species which she belonged to died out about 2.5 million years ago.

Lucy was not a human, but most scientists agree that she may have been a recent ancestor of humans.

Lucy's brain was bigger than the brains of the primates who were her ancestors, but much smaller than a human brain today. She was more intelligent than the primates, but less intelligent than us.

Her brain was less than one third the size of a modern human brain.

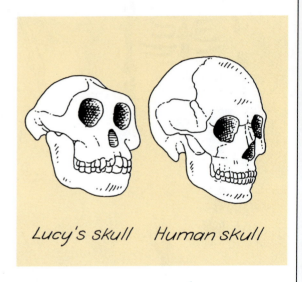

Lucy's skull   Human skull

Lucy would not have been able to think, as we do today, but she did know who were her enemies and where to hide from them. She also knew where and when she could find food and she knew her own family group. This was important, because she lived with them and they all needed to help each other.

Lucy could not speak as we can speak to each other today. She did not use language because her brain had not developed well enough.

What did Lucy look like?

Lucy was an adult female. She was probably about 25 years old when she died.

Lucy's bones were thick, and she probably had big, strong muscles. Her arms were rather long as the picture here shows.

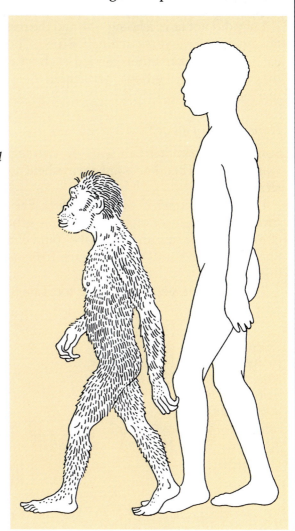

Lucy was about 1.25 metres tall and weighed about 30 kilograms. She was the same size as a six-year-old child today, so she was much smaller than human adults. Lucy had a low forehead, a flat nose and no chin. She had a large jaw and very big back teeth.

How did Lucy live?

Lucy lived with about 40 other primates in a group. Some of the others were her relatives. Her own parents were probably with the group until they died, and her own children stayed in the group, too.

Lucy ate fruit, nuts, leaves, berries and eggs. She had large flat teeth to grind anything hard. If she found the body of a dead bird or animal she probably ate that as well.

Lucy did not have a home. She and the rest of her group were always on the move, searching for food. They probably helped each other. Perhaps they carried each other's children when they were young. Perhaps they shared their food if one of them was sick.

How did Lucy move?

Some other primates can walk on two legs, but they cannot walk upright. Their knees are always bent and their legs are not straight.

Lucy walked upright on straight legs, like humans today. She probably spent most of her time on the ground, but she could climb too. If she saw an enemy she could climb a tree to escape. She could also climb trees to reach fruits and berries in high branches.

She may have slept in the trees too, safe from her enemies.

This picture shows the difference between Lucy's skeleton and the skeleton of an ape.

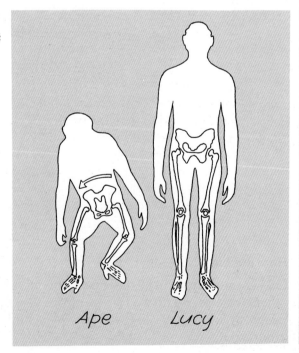

Why did Lucy walk upright?

The primates who were Lucy's ancestors lived in the trees. They ate fruit, leaves, nuts, berries and perhaps a few insects and lizards. They moved through the trees easily because they had long, strong arms to climb and swing.

Scientists do not yet understand exactly why Lucy's species left the trees and started to live on the ground and walk upright.

Some scientists think that it was because of food. About four million years ago the Earth's climate became much drier and the forests began to die. Grassland took the place of the forests. Perhaps it was difficult for the primates who lived in the trees to find food at that time. They may have left the forests to search for food in the grasslands.

Once on the grassland primates did not need to climb and swing. But they had to
- travel a long way to find food.
- stand upright to gather nuts, berries and fruit from low bushes.
- cross rivers or see over tall grass.

For all these things it was probably better to walk on two legs than on four.

Other scientists have different ideas. They think that Lucy's species walked upright because in that way they could care better for their babies.

Primates do not have many babies. This means that they have to be very careful that their babies do not die.

Perhaps it was easier for Lucy's species to care for their babies on the ground than in the trees. If Lucy lived in the trees she might drop her baby, or it might fall. If this happened on the ground the baby would not be hurt. On the ground other primates in the group could help to feed the babies.

Some scientists do not agree with either of these ideas. They think that Lucy's species started to walk upright because they were using their arms to carry things. Perhaps they carried their food away to eat it quietly in a safe place. Perhaps they carried their babies safely in their arms. If they were carrying things in their arms then they had to walk upright on their legs.

We know that Lucy walked upright because we have her hip and leg bones. We know how they fit together. But these are not all that we have. Scientists have also found fossil footprints of her species.

The Story of the Footprints

It was the end of the dry season. There were clouds overhead, but it had not rained for months.

Forty kilometres away the Sadiman volcano was stirring, as it often did. It threw clouds of grey ash into the air. The ash later covered the ground for miles around.

Late one afternoon a few spots of rain fell. There was just enough rain to make the grey ash a little bit wet.

After the rain stopped the animals returned. Elephants, pigs, deer, a tiger and dozens of monkeys left their footprints in the wet ash. Luckily there was no wind, so the ash did not blow away.

The next morning a family group came to the same place. A large male went first, walking to the north. A smaller female followed him. She placed her feet in the footprints left by the male. At her side ran a child. At one point the child stopped and turned to the left. They all left their footprints in the ash.

After the family had passed the sun baked the footprints hard. More ash covered them soon afterwards. In time they were buried deep under layers of dust, ash and silt.

Nobody saw the footprints for more than 3.5 million years. Then they were found, by good luck, at Laetoli in Tanzania in 1976. The fossil footprints are very much like human footprints today.

This picture shows the footprints found at Laetoli. The footprints on the right were made by an ancestor of the horse.

Part 4

Handy-man

Lake Turkana in Kenya is over 160 kilometres long and lies in a dry, stony desert. The sun beats down every day, and for most of the year the lake and the land around seem dead.

When it rains, however, things are different. Flowers grow. Dry river beds suddenly fill with water. Deep gullies are cut by rushing streams.

Lake Turkana was not always like this. Millions of years ago it was much larger than it is today, and the climate was much wetter. Fast rivers carried sand and silt into the lake. Nearby volcanoes added their load of ash and dust. Thick layers of rock slowly built up.

Lake Turkana two million years ago

This is how Lake Turkana looked two million years ago. The river flowed from the mountains down into the lake. It dropped its load of sand and silt on the bed of the lake. Volcanoes added ash and dust.

- sediment deposited by the rivers
- volcanic rock
- streams which flow after heavy rain
- rivers

Lake Turkana today

Today no water flows into Lake Turkana, and it is dry. Streams which flow fast after heavy rain cut deep gullies into the old bed of the lake. Thousands of fossils have been found there.

One afternoon in summer 1972 a scientist, Bernard Ngeneo, was walking through a dry gully near Lake Turkana. Hundreds of other people had walked that way before. At the side of the path he noticed a few small pieces of bone. He stopped to look at them.

A minute later Bernard Ngeneo was holding in his hand some of the most interesting fossils ever found.

What did Bernard Ngeneo find?

Bernard Ngeneo and the other scientists working with him found over 300 small pieces of a fossil skull. Some of the pieces were as big as a matchbox. Others were smaller than a fingernail.

Over the next few weeks the scientists put all the pieces together. When they had finished they had a nearly complete skull. They could even see tiny fossil tooth marks on the skull, where a mouse had bitten into it.

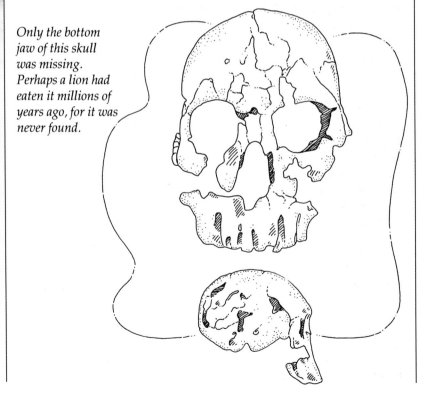

Only the bottom jaw of this skull was missing. Perhaps a lion had eaten it millions of years ago, for it was never found.

The scientists did not find the rest of the skeleton. They had, however, already found many other fossil bones from the same species at Lake Turkana and in Tanzania. Some fossils found in Ethiopia and South Africa are probably from the same species.

Now that Bernard Ngeneo had found the skull scientists knew much more about the species. They called it Handy-man.

What was Handy-man?

Handy-man was a species of primate which lived from 2 to 1.5 million years ago. Bernard Ngeneo's skull was about two million years old.

Handy-man was probably the first species of human, and our ancestor.

Handy-man's brain was bigger than Lucy's brain but smaller than ours. Handy-man was more intelligent than Lucy, but not as intelligent as us. Handy-man could think, though not nearly as well as humans today.

Handy-man's brain was not just bigger than Lucy's. It was also a different shape. Different parts of the brain control different things. The front part of a human brain controls the way we see. The back part controls the way we move. The part of the brain which controls speech is in the middle. In Lucy's brain this part was not developed at all. In Handy-man's brain this part was just starting to develop.

Handy-man's throat could probably not make as many sounds as a human throat today, but language of some sort may have begun. Handy-man could make sounds or even speak a few easy words which his friends could understand.

What did Handy-man look like?

Handy-man was 1.2 to 1.5 metres high and weighed about 50 kilograms. Handy-man had thick bones and was very strong. Handy-man's face was smaller, narrower and longer than Lucy's, but still had a large forehead and flat nose. The jaws and teeth were also big and strong.

Handy-man walked upright and had arms which were a little shorter than Lucy's. His hands and feet were very much like ours. Handy-man had wide hips, so that females of the species could have babies with large heads.

Where did Handy-man live?

Handy-man needed water to drink, so lived near rivers, lakes and streams.
Handy-man probably lived in a place like this.

Two million years ago the climate at Lake Turkana (and at the other places where Handy-man fossils have been found) was much wetter than it is today. The lake was much bigger, and there were shady trees nearby. It was a good place for Handy-man to live.

When Handy-man looked around he saw some of the ancestors of the birds, fish and animals which live in Africa today. The lakes and rivers were home for the ancestors of our elephants, lions, cattle and giraffes.

How did Handy-man live?

Handy-man lived in family groups of about 25. Parents and children probably stayed in the same group for the whole of their lives. Young males perhaps joined other groups to find partners.

Handy-man ate much the same food as Lucy. He gathered nuts, berries, fruits and eggs. If he found a dead animal he might eat that too. Perhaps Handy-man even hunted small animals such as pigs or deer himself.

Handy-man's tools

Scientists gave Handy-man his name because he was the first species to use his hands and make tools.

As well as fossil bones scientists have also found hundreds of Handy-man's fossil tools.

The first tools were probably sharp sticks and pieces of bark. Handy-man used the sticks to dig up roots and the bark to make a tray to carry nuts or fruit, but nothing is left of them. The earliest tools have disappeared.

Stone is different however. It does not rot away, but lasts for millions of years.

Handy-man probably found stones and used them to break open nuts or even animal bones.

About two million years ago Handy-man began to shape stones to make better tools. When Handy-man hit one stone hard against another, one stone broke. He could then use the hard, sharp edge of the broken stone to cut up meat.

Later Handy-man made tools with different shapes.

Handy-man picked up a stone like this from the bed of a river. Then he used it to break open the leg bone of a deer.

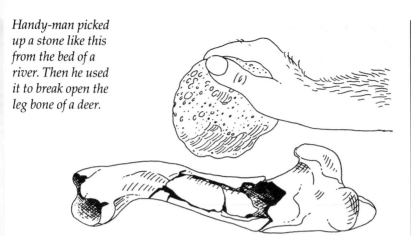

Stones like this have a sharp edge all round for cutting meat from animal bones.

This stone can scrape meat off animal skins.

In East Africa most fossil tools are made of lava. Some lava choppers and scrapers have been found ten miles away from the rocks from which they were made. Handy-man must have carried some tools around.

Handy-man's camp sites

Thousands of fossils have been found at some sites in Tanzania.

Handy-man did not live in one place, but he probably stayed at camp sites for days or even weeks. At the camp sites he gathered food, made tools, and killed animals or fish to eat. Scientists have found pieces of fossil bone from giraffes, pigs, deer, wildebeeste and other animals, and the tools which Handy-man used to kill and cut them up.

Handy-man may have built the first houses at these camp sites. Scientists have found old stone circles with big stones which were probably used to hold down branches for hut walls. Fossil tools and pieces of bone have also been found in such places. They show that Handy-man made tools and cut up meat here.

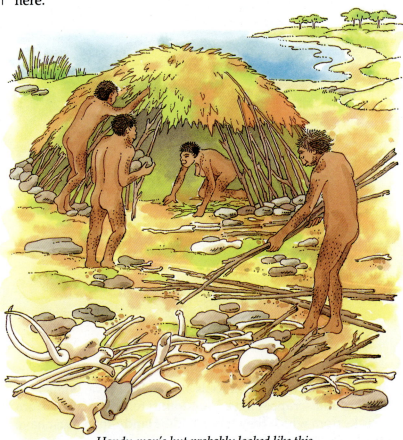

Handy-man's hut probably looked like this.

Part
5

The Turkana Boy

A Sad Story

"Stay here," his father had told him the day before. "Danger."

The boy did not listen. Early next morning, while the family slept, he slipped away. The boy hurried to the river. The water was low but he had seen fish there.

The river flowed at the bottom of a deep gully. The boy climbed down the steep sides, half sliding, half falling.

Then he was standing in the clear water. Now for the fish. He held a heavy stone in his hand. If he could just catch one of the slow-swimming fish he would beat it on the head and kill it. Then his mother would be very happy.

The boy was thinking so hard about the fish that he did not hear the noise. It got louder and louder. Nearer and nearer it came, and still the boy did not hear.

He never really knew what happened. Suddenly the water crashed over him. The sides of the valley were too steep. The trees were too high. He could not get away from the flood.

He screamed but nobody heard. He fought as the water swept him along. It was no good.

The boy died quickly in the rushing water.

The flood carried the boy's body many miles away to the edge of the lake. There it dropped him in the soft mud.

He never did find the fish, but the fish found him. Soon nothing was left of the boy but his bones.

The boy's bones were soon covered by a thin layer of silt. As time passed more and more layers of silt built up. Dust and ash were added by a nearby volcano, and the waters of the lake itself rose and fell.

The layers of silt, ash and dust, and the boy's bones turned into hard rock.

The hunt for the fossils

1.6 million years later a Kenyan scientist, Kamoya Kimeu, was searching for fossils near Lake Turkana.

One day Kimeu crossed a sandy, dried-up river bed. As he kicked at some small black lava stones he spotted a tiny fossil. He knew at once that it came from a skull.

Over the next weeks Kimeu and the other scientists in the camp searched for more fossils. It was hard, hot, dusty work. They had to search through tons of soil, rocks and stones.

Kimeu always started work early in the morning, before it was too hot. He explained some of the problems.

"We drive to the area we want to search, and then walk in twos: there's always a danger of lions or snake bites or something like that. And when someone finds something they can discuss it with their partner. It takes about three years before you know the fossils very well.

"It's easy if the fossil is grey or white because you can see it from 20 yards. But mostly the fossils are very dark and then it's difficult. If we find something interesting, we get on our hands and knees to be very near the ground. You can see very small pieces then."

What did the scientists find?

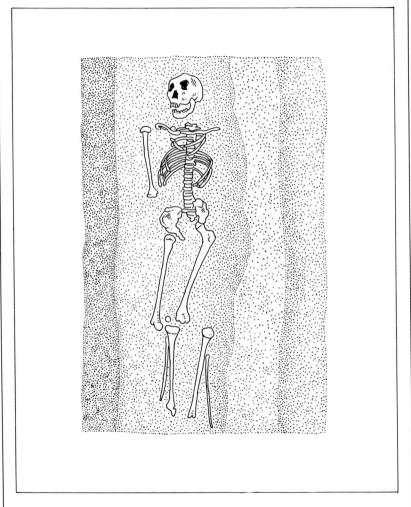

They found an almost complete fossil skeleton, with arms, legs, backbone, ribs, hips and shoulder bone, skull and jaws. The skull was broken into 70 tiny pieces, but the scientists put it together again.

What was the Turkana boy?

The Turkana boy belonged to a species which died out about 200,000 years ago, but this species was the ancestor of humans today.

The Turkana boy lived 1.6 million years ago. His skeleton was found in Kenya. Other fossils from the same species have been found in Tanzania, Ethiopia, South Africa and Algeria.

The Turkana boy was about 12 years old when he died. We know this because his second teeth were just coming through.

If the Turkana boy had grown up his brain would not have been as big as the brain of a human today. It would have been much bigger than Lucy's brain or Handy-man's brain. The Turkana boy was almost as intelligent as us.

The part of Turkana boy's brain which controls speech had not developed very much, but he could speak and understand language.

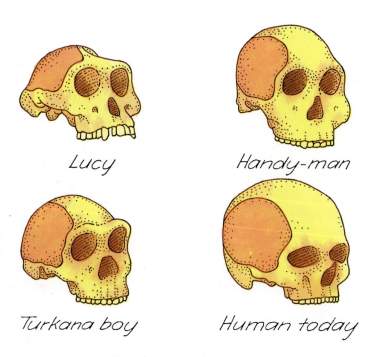

This picture shows the skulls of Lucy, Handy-man, Turkana boy and a human today. Can you see how they are different?

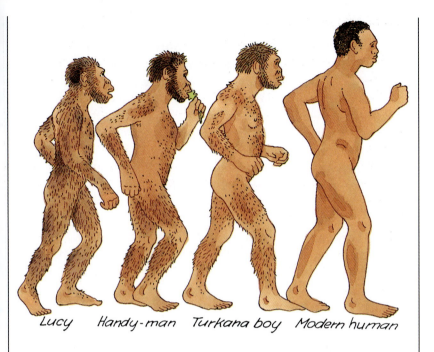

This picture shows the difference in size between Lucy, Handy-man, Turkana boy and a human of today.

What did the Turkana boy look like?

The Turkana boy was 1.6 metres tall and weighed about 40 kilograms. If he had lived to become an adult, he would have been about 1.8 metres tall and would have weighed 50 – 70 kilograms. He would have been nearly as big as an adult male today.

The Turkana boy looked very much like any boy reading this book. His body was almost exactly the same, except that he had bigger muscles at the back of his neck and across his shoulders. He needed these muscles to hold up his head, which was front-heavy.

The Turkana boy's head was different from a boy's head today. His skull was much thicker, and was long and low. He had heavy eyebrows, a big jaw, but no chin.

The Turkana boy's skin was dark so that the sun did not burn him, but it was not hairy.

How did the Turkana boy live?

The Turkana boy lived in a family group of 25 to 50 people. The group did not have a real home, but moved from place to place in search of food. Sometimes, however, the group stayed at one camp site for a few days. Then they could gather fruits and nuts, cut up meat into smaller pieces, sleep and rest, drink from the nearby rivers and lakes, make new tools from stone, wood and bone, and plan the next hunt.

The Turkana boy ate nuts, berries, birds' eggs and fruit, just as Handy-man did. He probably ate more roots. The soil on the roots made marks and scratches on his teeth which can still be seen.

The Turkana boy ate more meat than Handy-man. Perhaps he found dead animals as he travelled round, but he probably hunted with his father and the other adults in his family group.

The Turkana boy knew how to make and use stone tools, and his tools were much better than Handy-man's. His species made the first hand-axes and cleavers. The Turkana boy could knock tiny flakes from both sides of a stone and make sharp cutting edges. The flakes themselves were very sharp and could cut animal hides.

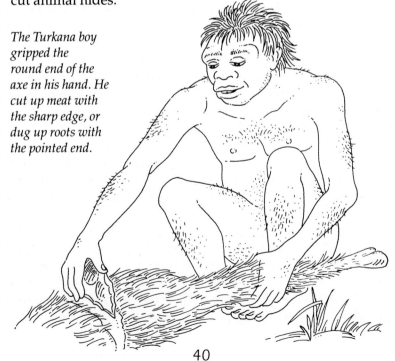

The Turkana boy gripped the round end of the axe in his hand. He cut up meat with the sharp edge, or dug up roots with the pointed end.

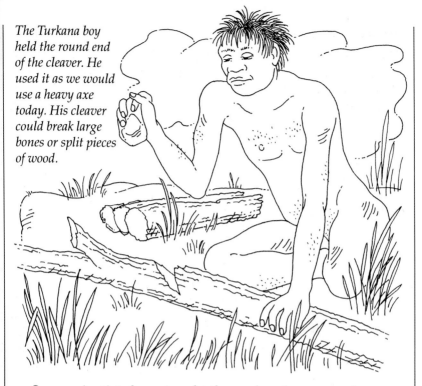

The Turkana boy held the round end of the cleaver. He used it as we would use a heavy axe today. His cleaver could break large bones or split pieces of wood.

Some scientists have taught themselves how to make stone tools today. The tools are so good that the scientists have cut up an elephant with them.

Small stone flakes can cut through the elephant's hide, which is two centimetres thick. Hand-axes can cut the elephant's muscles. One scientist cut up nearly 50 kilograms of meat in an hour with stone tools. Afterwards his tools were so dull that they could not cut any more.

At Olorgesailie, in Kenya, scientists found a very old site where the Turkana boy's species had hunted. Long ago Olorgesailie was a lake, although it is now dry. Many animals came to drink and eat at the lake, and left thousands of fossils behind.

Scientists found the fossil bones of 60 big baboons at this site. They also found more than 10,000 hand-axes which had killed the baboons. It would have been difficult to kill the baboons. Some of them were as big and heavy as humans today. Their killers must have planned the hunt and worked together so that everything went right.

The Turkana boy's life was much easier than Handy-man's. He had better tools, and perhaps he also had fire. Handy-man knew about fire started by lightning. The Turkana boy's species knew how to keep fires going. With fire he could cook food. He could keep warm on cold nights. He could drive away wild animals.

Human travels

Africa was a very good place for our ancestors to live. There were plenty of places where the climate was warm but not too hot. There was water to drink. There were nuts, fruit, berries and other food from plants growing all year round. There were plenty of animals to hunt.

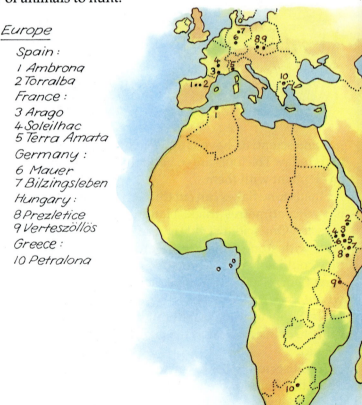

Europe

Spain:
1 Ambrona
2 Torralba

France:
3 Arago
4 Soleilhac
5 Terra Amata

Germany:
6 Mauer
7 Bilzingsleben

Hungary:
8 Prezletice
9 Verteszöllös

Greece:
10 Petralona

This map shows sites where fossils of Turkana boy's species have been found.

But even though Africa was such a good place to live, some of the Turkana boy's species left the continent. Very slowly they travelled great distances until they reached the furthest parts of the Earth.

Scientists do not know why humans moved to other parts of the Earth. Perhaps they did not even know what they were doing. After all, Lucy, Handy-man and the Turkana boy all spent their lives moving around. If the Turkana boy's species only moved 80 kilometres in a hundred years, they would still travel from Nairobi to Peking in less than 10,000 years.

Fossils from the Turkana boy's species have been found in China, India, Java and Europe, but they are all much younger than the fossils from Africa.

Asia

  India :
  1 Narmada
  China :
  2 Peking
  3 Lantian
  4 Nanzhao
  5 Yunxi
  6 Hexian
  7 Yuanmou
  8 Luc Yen
  Indonesia :
  9 Sangiran
  10 Perning/Modjokerto
  11 Trinil

Africa

  Algeria :
  1 Ternifine
  Kenya :
  2 Melka Kunture
  3 Omo River
  4 Nariokotome
  5 Koobi Fora
  6 Lake Turkana
  7 Chesowanja
  8 Olorgesailie
  Tanzania :
  9 Olduvai Gorge
  South Africa :
  10 Swartkrans

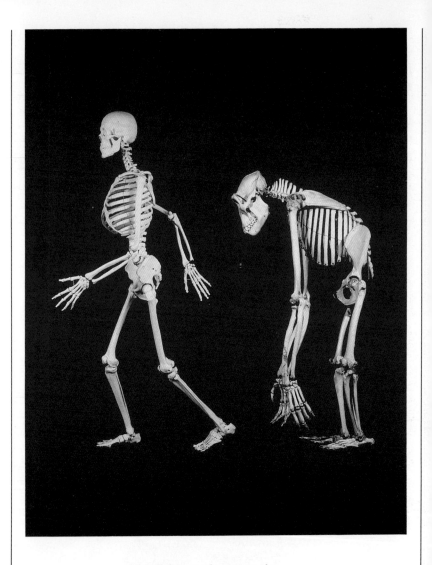

*The skeletons of a man and an ape.
What differences can you see?*

Finding out more about fossils

The oldest fossils of humans and their ancestors have all been found in Africa. The oldest human fossils from Europe are only 500,000 years old, and from Asia only 700,000 years old.

Scientists believe that the ancestors of all the humans living on the Earth today came from Africa.

Although scientists have found many fossils they still do not know exactly how humans today have evolved. Lucy was probably the ancestor of Handy-man. Handy-man was probably the ancestor of the Turkana boy. The Turkana boy was probably the ancestor of humans today. But until more fossils are found nobody can be quite sure.

If you are interested in humans and evolution perhaps you could be a fossil hunter yourself. Perhaps you could find the missing fossils which will tell us exactly what happened in the past.

You may also be able to go and see some of the fossils in this book.

- Lucy is kept in the National Museum of Ethiopia, Addis Ababa, Ethiopia.
- Bernard Ngeneo's Handy-man skull is kept in the National Museum of Kenya, Nairobi, Kenya.
- The Turkana boy is also kept in the National Museum of Kenya, Nairobi, Kenya.
- Other interesting fossils of humans and their ancestors are kept in the National Museum of Tanzania, Dar es Salaam, Tanzania, and the Transvaal Museum, Pretoria, South Africa.
- You can visit sites where scientists are searching for human fossils at Olorgesailie and Kariandusi in Kenya.

Already available in **Mactracks**

Starters

The Hunter's Dream   Meja Mwangi
Martha's Mistakes   Lorna Evans
Martha's Big News   Lorna Evans
Fiki Learns to Like Other People   Lauretta Ngcobo
Zulu Spear   Olive Langa
Mercy in a Hurry   Mary Harrison
Tanzai and Bube   John Haynes
Karabo's Accident   Frances Cross
The Little Apprentice Tailor   Marcus Kamara
Follow that Footprint!   Jill Inyundo
We're Still Moving!   Damian Morgan

Sprinters

Mystery of the Sagrenti Treasure   Ekow Yarney
Eyes and Ears   Brenda Ferry
Eyes and Ears Work Hard   Brenda Ferry
One in a Million   Emma Johnson
Map on the Wall   Colin Swatridge
Magic Trees   Jenny Vincent
Dark Blue is for Dreams   Rosina Umelo
Danger in the Palace   Grace Nkansa
The Past Tells a Story   Lorna Evans (*non-fiction*)

Runners

Guitar Wizard   Walije Gondwe
Star   Nandi Dlovu
Days of Silence   Rosina Umelo
Never Leave Me   Hope Dube
Juwon's Battle   Victor Thorpe
Fineboy   Maurice Sotabinda
Front Page Story   John Byrne

Winners

Halima   Meshack Asare
Foli Fights the Forgers   Kofi Quaye
Jojo in New York   Kofi Quaye
Presents from Mr Bakare   Mary Harrison
Sara's Friends   Rosina Umelo
Trouble in the City   Hope Dube
Sunbird's Paradise   James Ngumy
Kayo's House   Barbara Kimenye
Be Beautiful   Lydia Eagle and Barbara Jackson (*non-fiction*)
Sport in Africa   Ossie Stuart (*non-fiction*)